ISBN-13: 978-1-64001-036-9
ISBN-10: 1-64001-036-X

FREE DOWNLOAD

www.papeteriebleu.com/tacolife

YOUR DOWNLOAD CODE: TL3935

@papeteriebleu

Papeterie Bleu

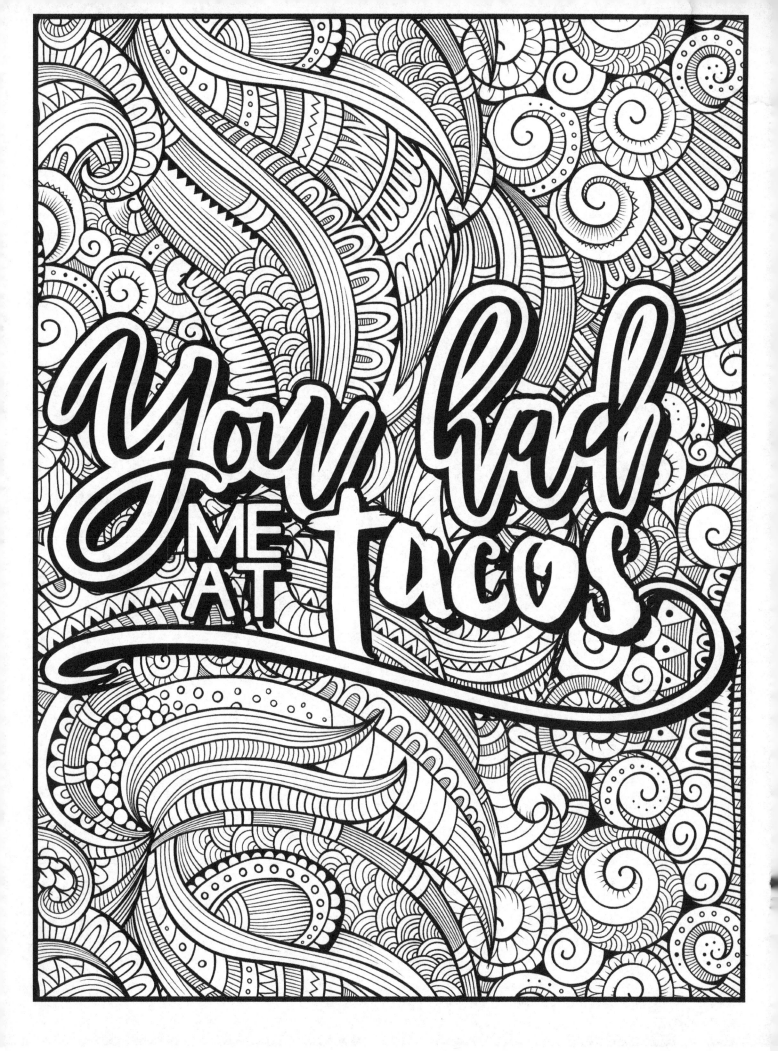

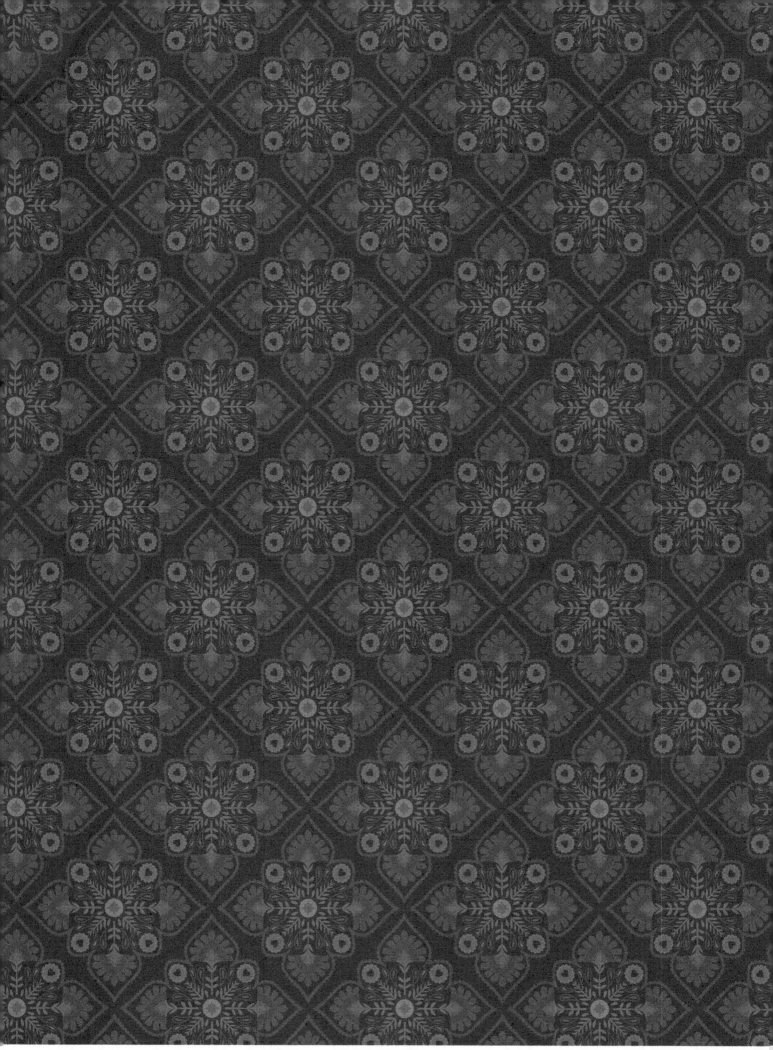

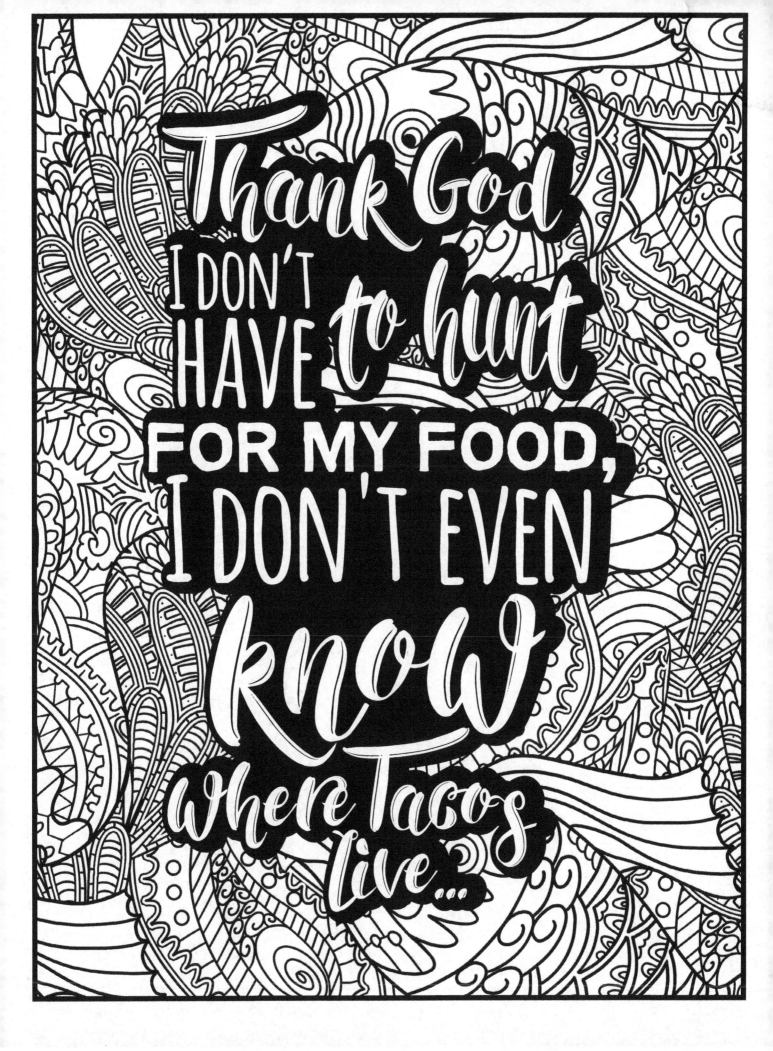

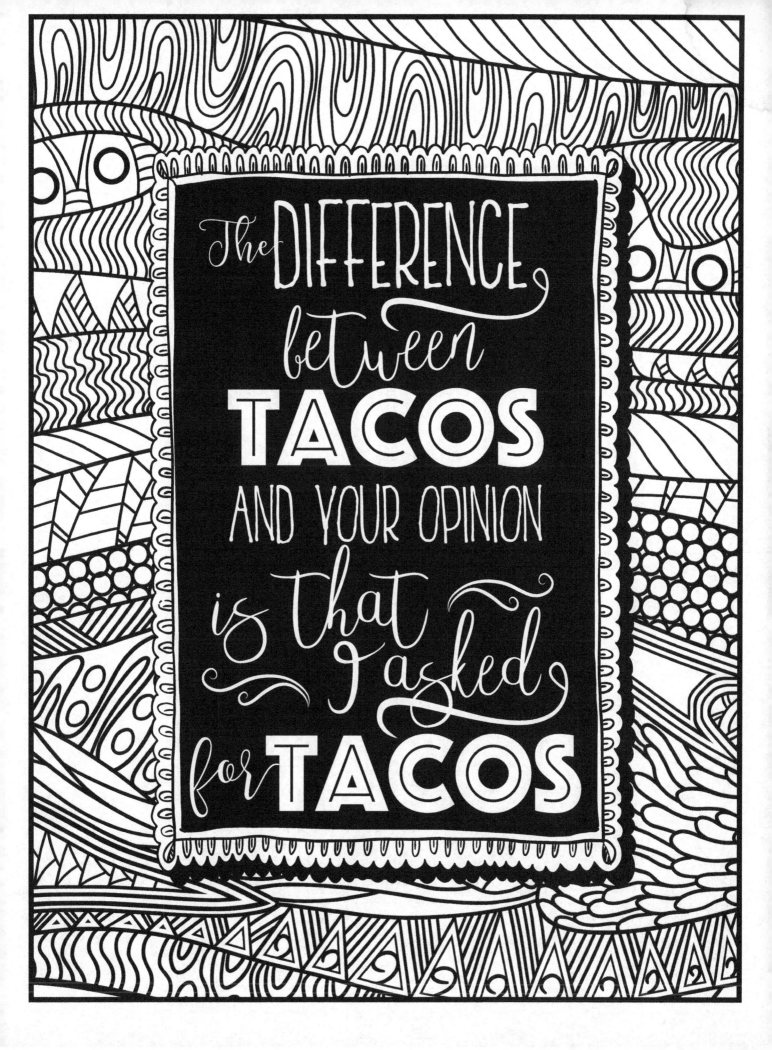

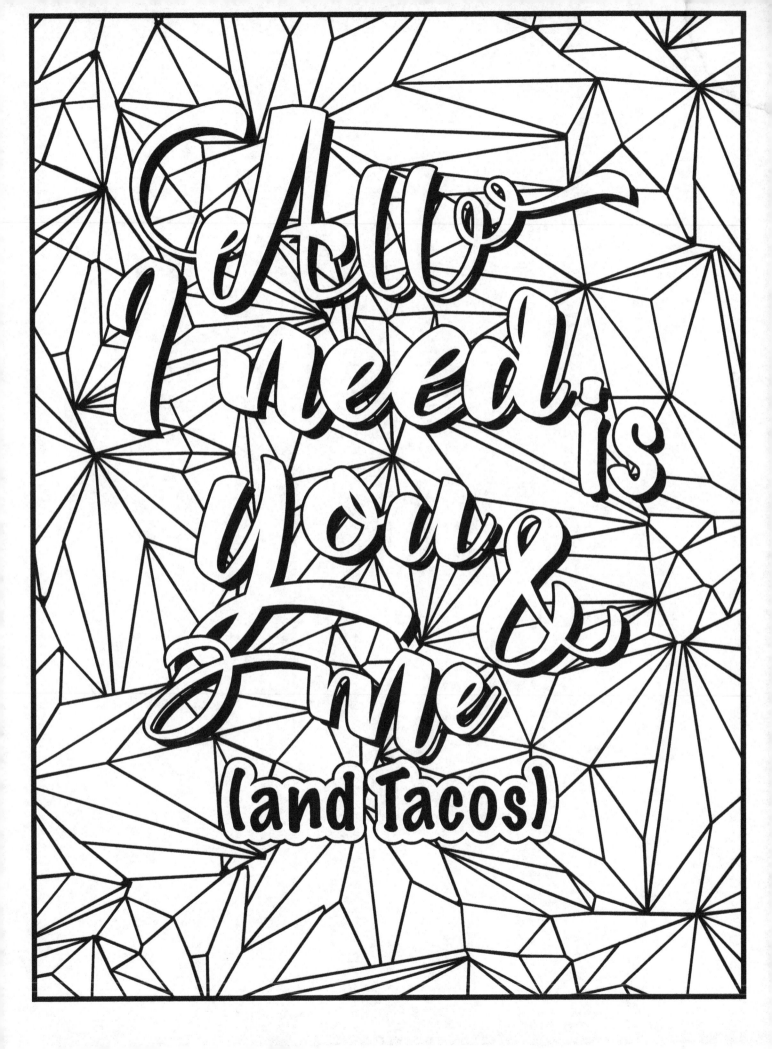

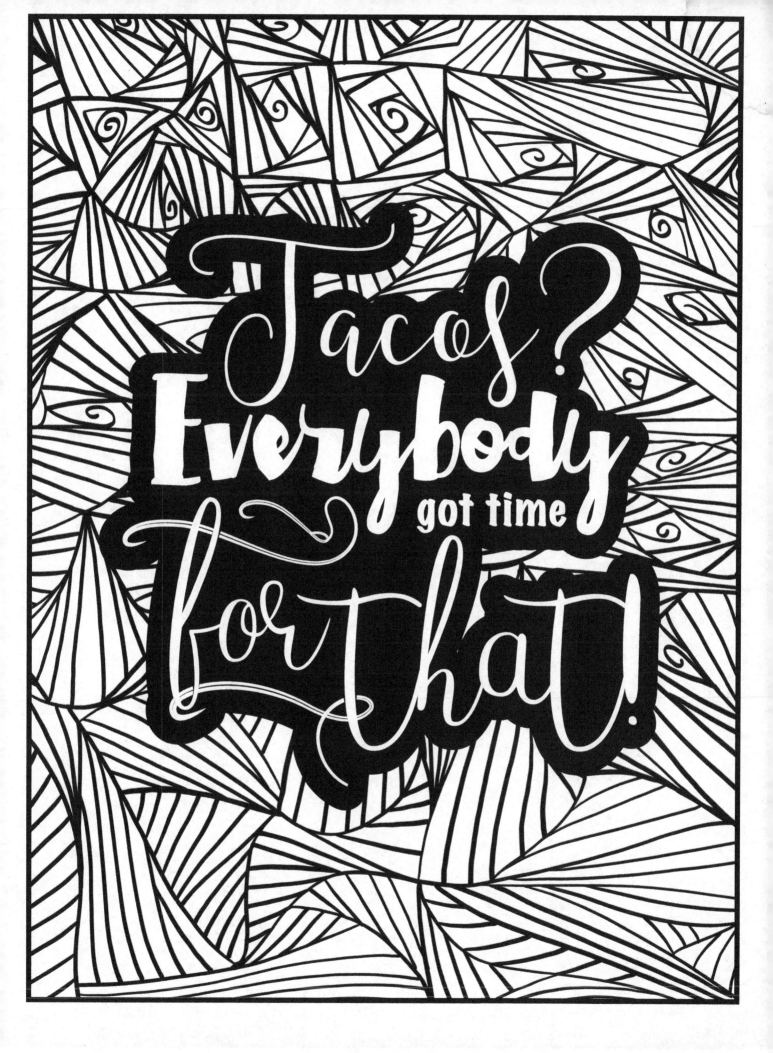

WHEN SOMEONE THINKS
I'M PAYING ATTENTION
TO WHAT THEY'RE SAYING
BUT
REALLY,
I'M JUST
THINKING
ABOUT
TACOS

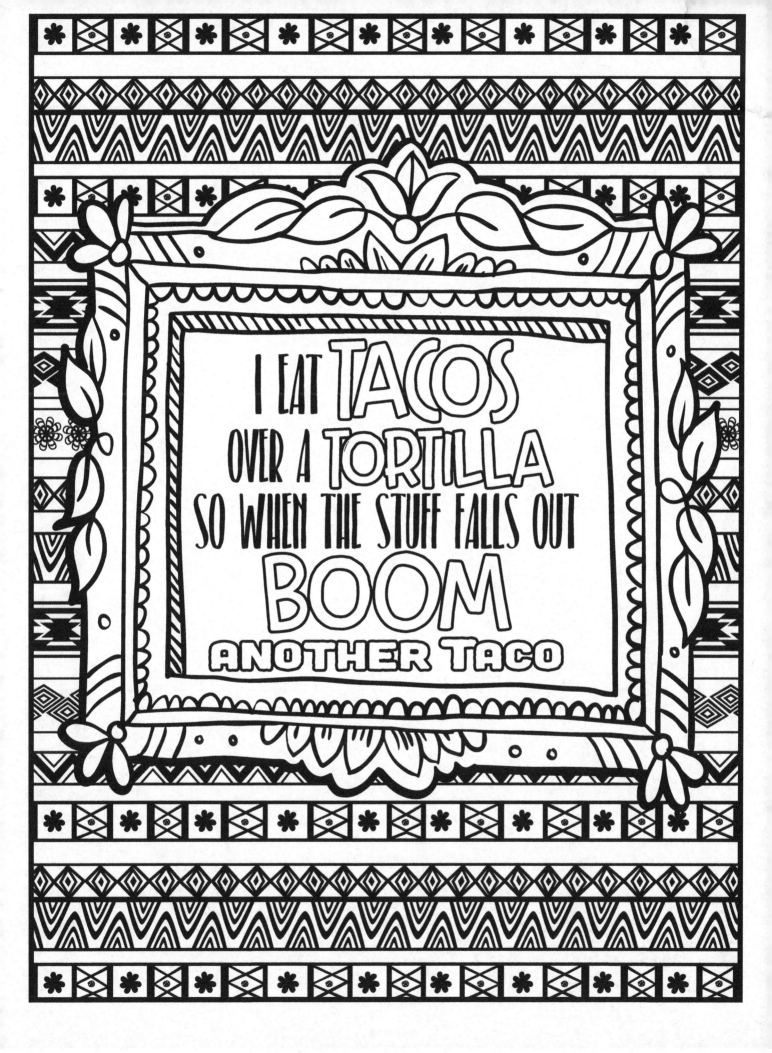

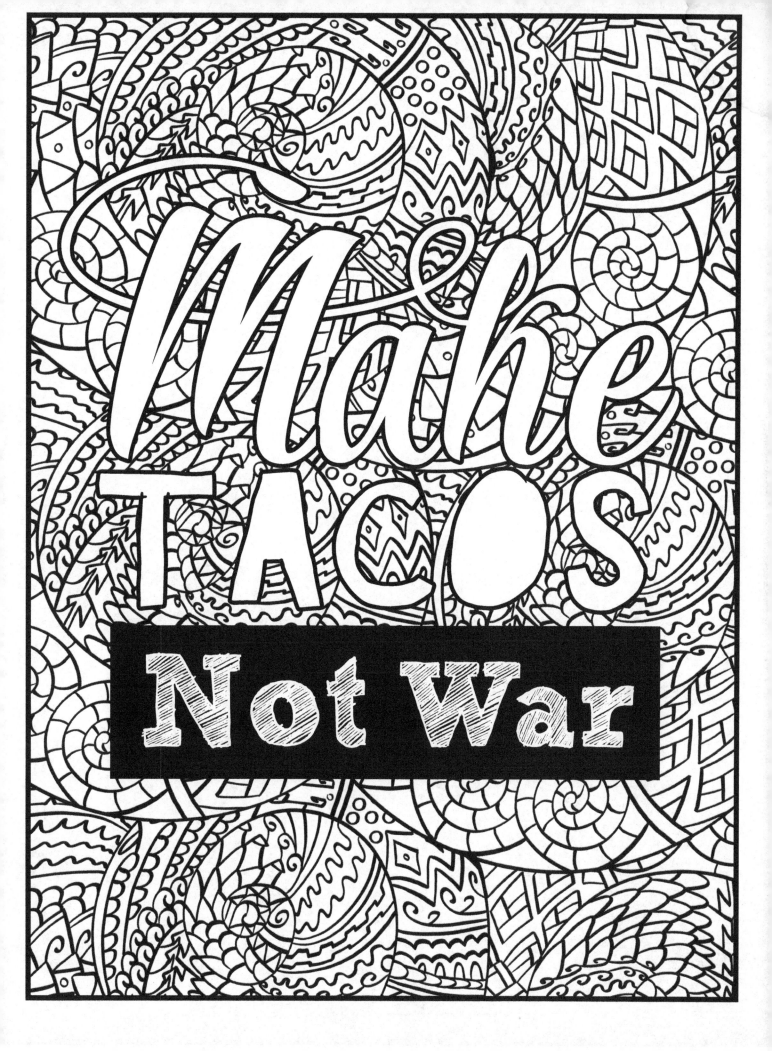

Don't trust PEOPLE THAT DISLIKE TACOS. They're probably NOT HUMAN.

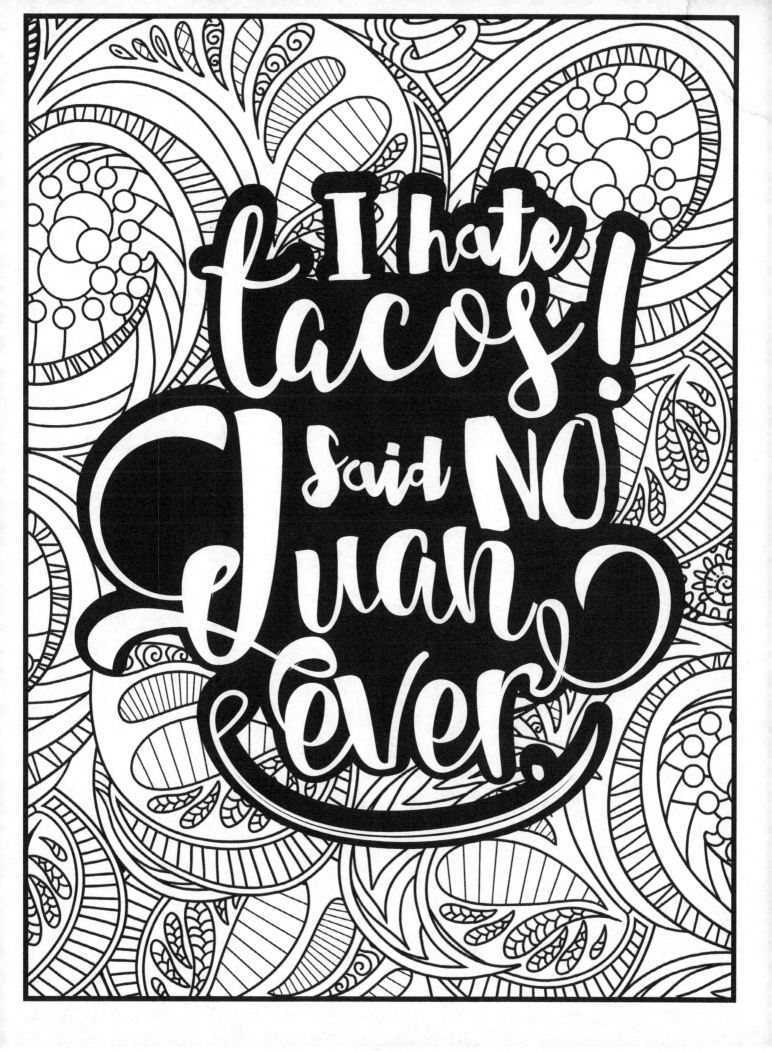

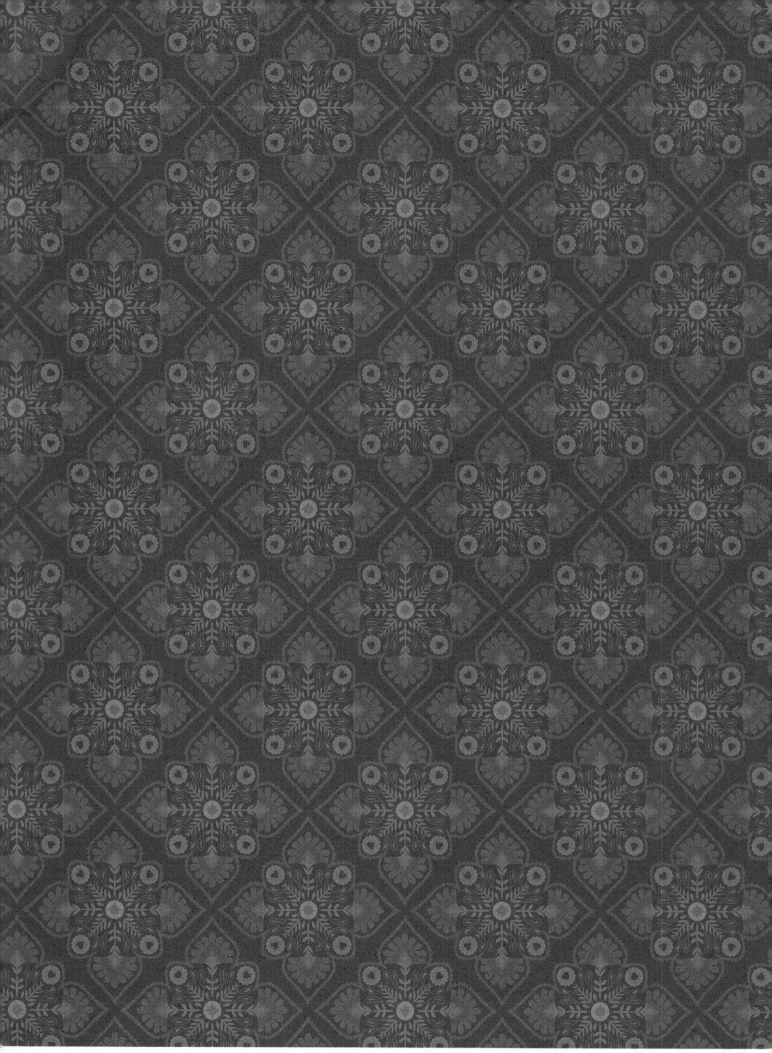

I wish
I WAS FULL OF
tacos
INSTEAD
OF
emotions

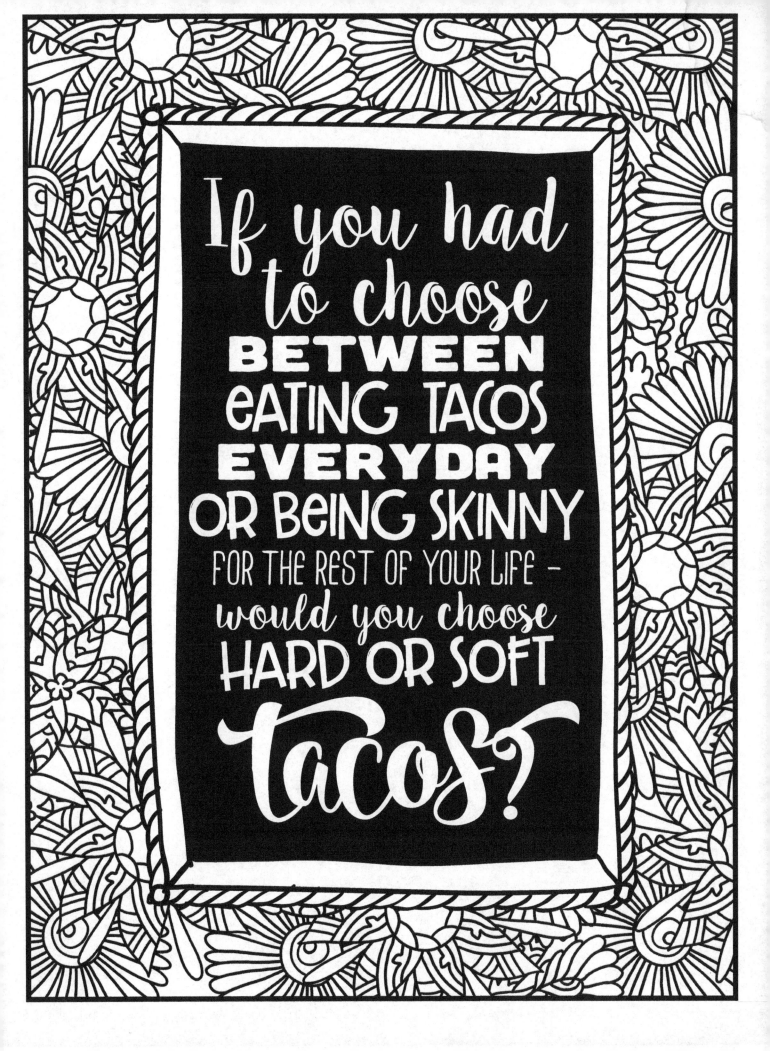

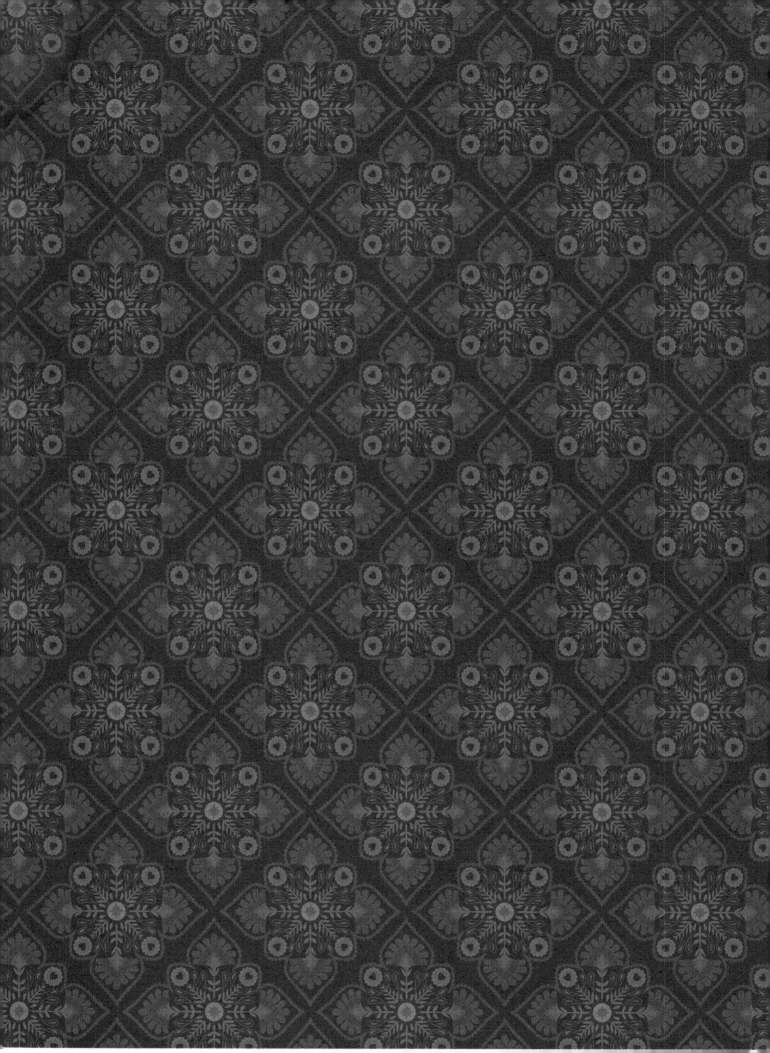

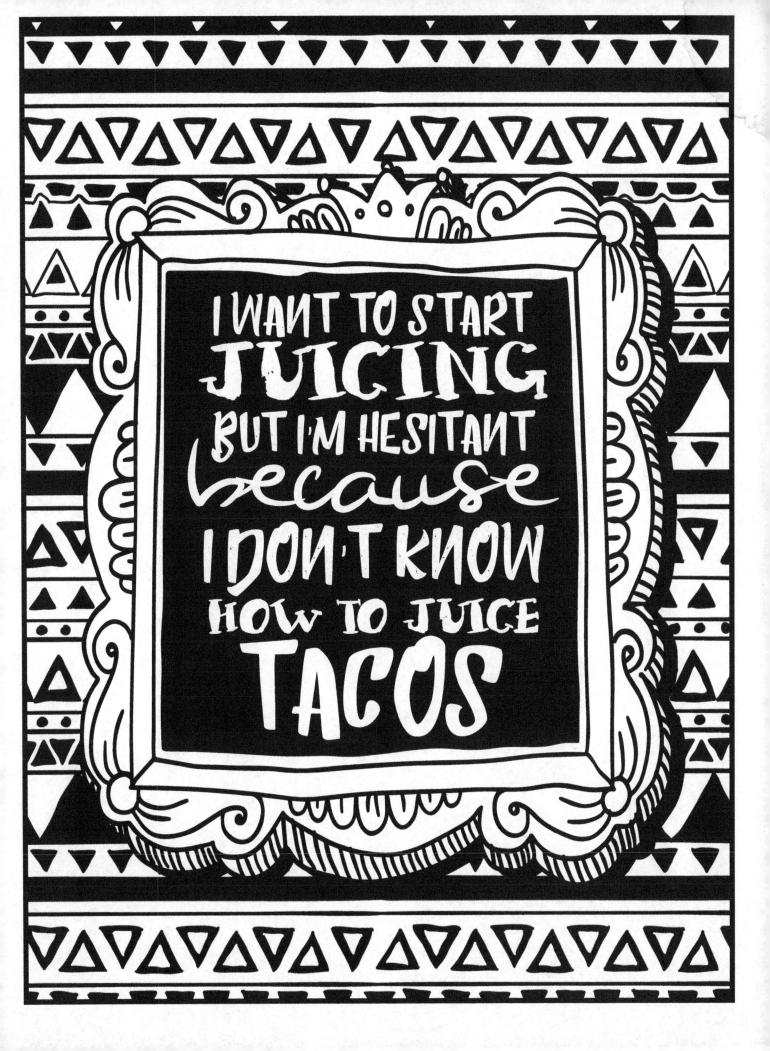

BE SURE TO FOLLOW US ON SOCIAL MEDIA FOR THE LATEST NEWS, SNEAK PEEKS, & GIVEAWAYS

@PapeterieBleu

Papeterie Bleu

@PapeterieBleu

ADD YOURSELF TO OUR MONTHLY NEWSLETTER FOR FREE DIGITAL DOWNLOADS AND DISCOUNT CODES

www.papeteriebleu.com/newsletter

CHECK OUT OUR OTHER BOOKS!

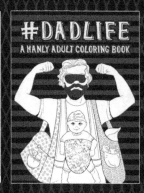
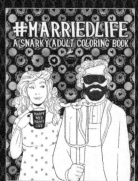

CHECK OUT OUR OTHER BOOKS!

www.papeteriebleu.com

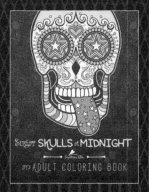

CHECK OUT OUR OTHER BOOKS!

www.papeteriebleu.com

  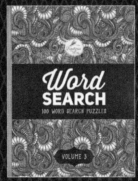 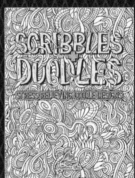 

    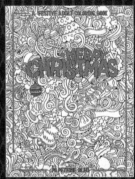

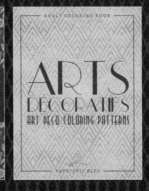